© 2010 by Parragon Books Ltd

This 2010 edition published by Sandy Creek,
by arrangement with Parragon.

Sandy Creek
122 Fifth Avenue
New York, NY 10011

ISBN-13: 978-1-4351-2351-9

Printed and bound in China

1 3 5 7 9 10 8 6 4 2

Disney

ALICE
in
WONDERLAND

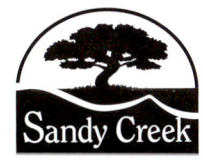

Sandy Creek

One summer day, a young girl named Alice found herself trapped in a history class. While her sister read about ancient kings, Alice put a daisy crown on her cat Dinah. The day was simply too splendid for classes, thought Alice.

"In my world, there would be no classes," said Alice to Dinah. "Everything would be nonsense."

As Alice dreamed of her wonderland, a well-dressed white rabbit ran past.

"I'm late! I'm late!" the White Rabbit cried. Alice raced after him. "He must be going to something really important, like a party," she told Dinah. They followed the White Rabbit to a rabbit hole.

Alice squeezed into the rabbit hole to follow him, even though she knew that curiosity often led to...

"TROUBBBBLLLE!" Alice's voice disappeared into a dark hole along with the rest of her. Alice floated down through the darkness, until she landed in a hallway.

She saw the White Rabbit disappearing down the hall in front of her.

"Oh, wait, Mister Rabbit, please!" Alice called. She raced down the hallway as the White Rabbit slammed a door behind him. Alice followed him through smaller and smaller doors. "Curiouser and curiouser," Alice said.

At the last and smallest door, Alice twisted the knob. A nose wiggled under her hand! What a strange place, Alice thought. She asked the Doorknob if she could go through. "Sorry," said the Doorknob. "You're much too big."

"Why don't you try the bottle on the table?" the Doorknob suggested.

A glass bottle labeled "Drink Me" appeared. With each sip, Alice shrank. Now she could fit through the door. But the door was locked!

17

Tiny Alice couldn't unlock the door. A magic
cookie made her into giant Alice, but giant Alice
couldn't fit through the door. Her tremendous
tears flooded the room. Alice shrank herself again,
and floated through the door's keyhole.

A wave swept Alice into a very odd race.
Fish and birds ran around a Dodo, trying
to get dry while the waves kept them wet.
Alice spotted the White Rabbit again.
"Mister Rabbit!" she called.

Alice chased the White Rabbit until she was deep in a wood. Instead of finding the White Rabbit, she found a pair of twins.

"I'm Tweedledee," said one. "I'm Tweedledum," said the other.

Alice told Tweedledee and Tweedledum, "I'm following the White Rabbit. I'm curious to know where he's going."

Tweedledum sighed. "Being curious can often lead to trouble" he said, waggling his finger at Alice.

Alice thanked them for the warning, but that didn't stop her rushing off to find the White Rabbit.

To Alice's surprise, the White Rabbit found her.
"I'm late!" he said. "Go get my gloves!"
Inside his cottage, Alice found cookies labeled "Eat
Me." Happily, Alice helped herself. Soon, she felt
herself growing…and growing…

...and growing, until her arms and legs stuck
out of the White Rabbit's cottage!

"HELP! Monster!" The White Rabbit ran to
fetch the Dodo.

The Dodo suggested burning down the house!

Alice ate a carrot from the Rabbit's garden and shrank to a tiny size once more. As the Dodo asked her for a match, the White Rabbit ran off again.

"Oh, dear," puffed tiny Alice, "I'll never catch him!"

Alice ran out of the garden and came upon a caterpillar making smoky vowels.

"Who are you?" he asked, puffing out a U.

Alice blew his smoke away—and blew the caterpillar right out of his clothes! He had become a big butterfly and started to fly off.

"One side of the mushroom will make you grow taller, and the other side will make you grow shorter," he said as he flew off.

Alice broke off two pieces of the mushroom. "I wonder which side is which," she said. With a shrug, Alice bit into the first mushroom piece.

She soon found out which piece made her grow, and she ate just the right amount to get back to her normal height.

Normal-sized again, Alice tucked the leftover mushroom pieces in her pocket. She searched for some sign of the White Rabbit. She did find signs, but they didn't help.

As Alice puzzled over which way to go, she heard singing.

Alice looked up and saw a
large mouth grinning down at her.
Bit by bit, the body of a Cheshire
Cat appeared.

"If you'd really like to know,"
he said, "the White Rabbit went
that way."

Alice walked on until she heard more singing. It was the Mad Hatter and the March Hare.

As the tea-for-twosome wished each other "Merry Unbirthday!" Alice tried to join them. But the pair shouted, "No room!"

The Mad Hatter swept off his hat and wished Alice a "Merry Unbirthday." There, on top of his head, was an unbirthday cake! "Now blow out the candle and make your wish," said the Mad Hatter.

As if in answer to Alice's wish, the White Rabbit appeared.

"I'm late!" he cried.

The Mad Hatter and the March Hare decided that the Rabbit's watch must be broken. So they fixed it with jam and lemon!

By now, Alice had had enough nonsense, and decided to find her way home.

Above her, Alice heard the Cheshire Cat again. "I want to go home," Alice told him.

The Cheshire Cat opened a door in the tree. Alice stepped through, into the world of the Queen of Hearts.

Alice heard royal trumpets sounding, which meant the
Queen of Hearts was nearby. Everybody seemed very nervous.
Suddenly she saw the White Rabbit dashing past her.

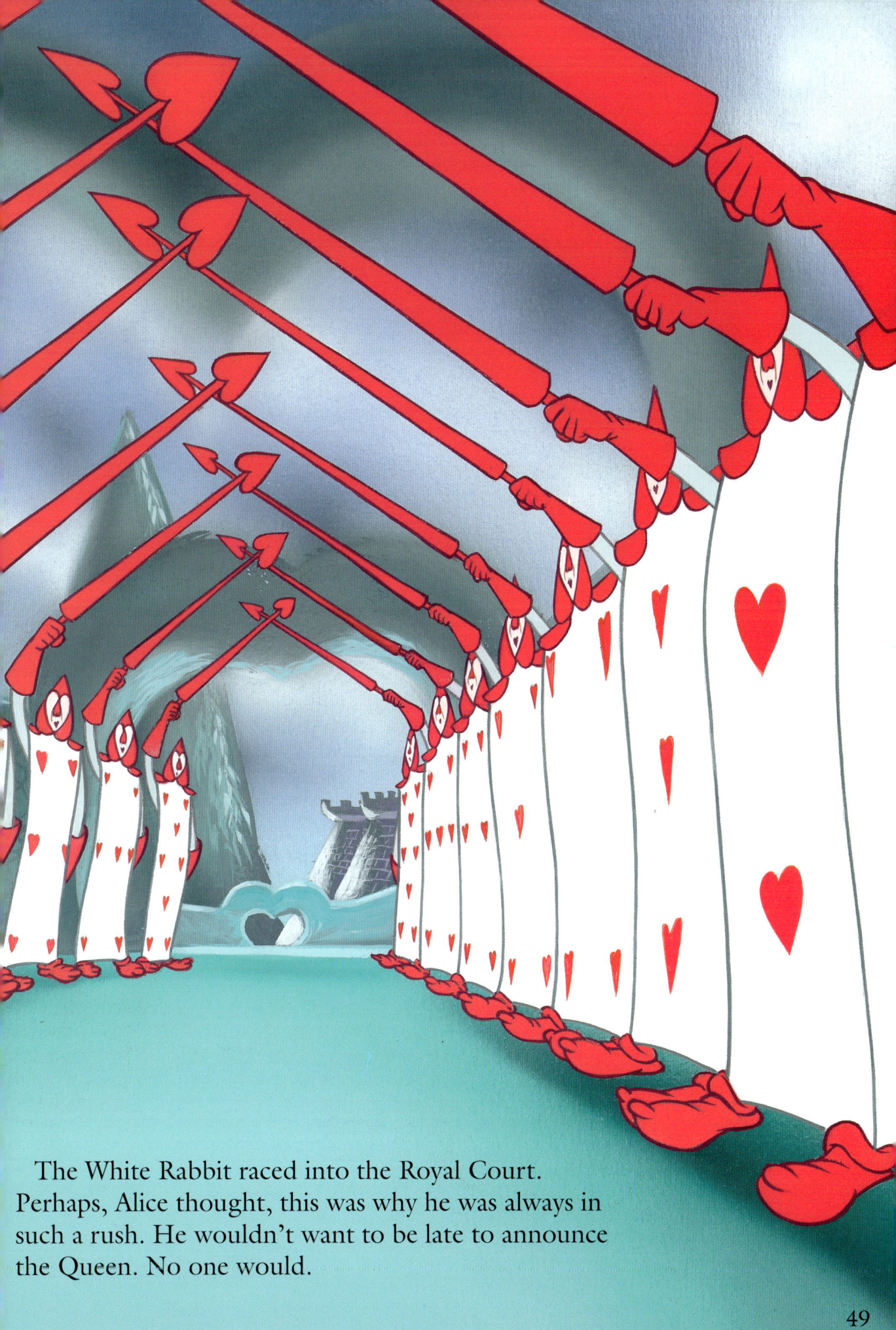

The White Rabbit raced into the Royal Court.
Perhaps, Alice thought, this was why he was always in
such a rush. He wouldn't want to be late to announce
the Queen. No one would.

"Her Imperial Highness!" called the White Rabbit. "The Queen of Hearts!"

The card courtiers cheered as the Queen entered. Trailing behind her, the King cleared his throat.

"And the King," the White Rabbit added.

The Queen spotted Alice. "Why, it's a little girl! Now where are you from and where are you going?"

"I'm trying to find my way home," Alice answered.

"Your way!" the Queen shouted. "All ways here are my ways!"

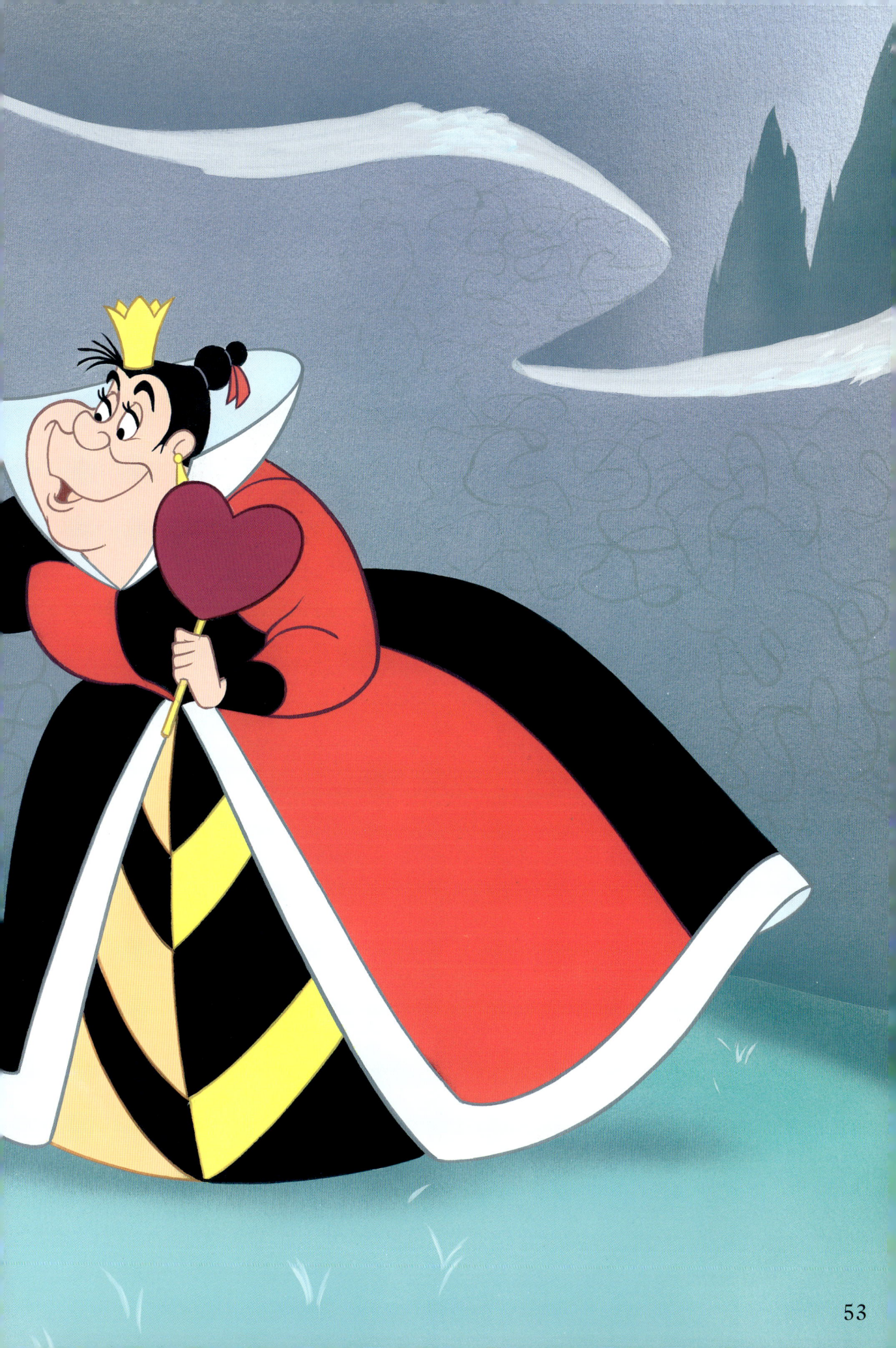

The Queen calmed down when she learned that
Alice played croquet. The Queen loved croquet.
The cards always made sure she won.

As the Queen prepared to swing, the Cheshire Cat
appeared. Only Alice could see him.

"You know," he told Alice, "we could make her really angry."

"Oh, no!" said Alice. "Stop!"

The Cheshire Cat tangled the Queen's skirt. She flopped over, and her skirt flapped up.

The Queen heaved herself up. "Someone's head will roll for this!" she bellowed at Alice. "Yours!"

The King pulled on the Queen's skirt. "Couldn't she have a little trial first?"

The Queen harumphed, but said yes.

The White Rabbit read the charge: Alice had caused the Queen of Hearts to lose her temper.

"Are you ready for your sentence?" the Queen asked Alice.

"Sentence?" said Alice. "Oh, but there must be a verdict first."

"Sentence first!" the Queen thundered.
"Off with her head!"

Alice found the mushroom pieces in her
pocket and stuck them in her mouth. She
grew until she towered over the Queen.

"I'm not afraid of you!" Alice said to
the Queen.

Suddenly, Alice felt herself shrinking!
"Off with her head!" the Queen shouted once more. The court of cards closed in on Alice. She raced away, into a maze. She managed to escape from the maze, and found herself back in the Dodo's beach race!

As Alice ran, she saw the Doorknob she had gone through earlier.

Alice tugged on the Doorknob. "I simply must get out!" she gasped.

"But you are outside," the Doorknob said.

Alice peered through the keyhole. There she was, sleeping in the meadow where she had had her history class!

"Alice!" Alice's sister woke her. "It's time for tea."

Alice looked around. Her wonderland—with its angry Queen—was gone.

Alice shook away her dream and smiled. The day was simply too splendid for nonsense!